To Sophie

VISTA

Printed in Hong Kong

Farrow Design

Published by Sanctuary Publishing Limited,
Sanctuary House, 45–53 Sinclair Road,
London W14 0NS, United Kingdom

Web site
www.sanctuarypublishing.com

Copyright
Andy Earl, 2000

Photographs
Courtesy Andy Earl

ISBN

Softback
1–86074–321–8

Hardback
1–86074–296–3

ANDY
EARL

Barbecue Chicken
1977

Foreword
Brian Clarke, Thailand, July 2000

In the 1970s, to be close to the real action in visual art, you had to be close to photography. Despite the rhetoric to the contrary, photography, until the Seventies, was a minor art that prided itself on a handful of major artists. Callahan, Frank, Siskind, Arbus and Evans were not the mighty names they are today, and Gibson, Clark and Sherman were rising stars in the rapidly-changing cosmos of the art world. British photography was still overwhelmed by the influence of Bill Brandt and David Bailey, but there was something in the air. Photography had come of age, the old debate about photography as art was now demonstrably redundant and, in the wake of American minimalist reductionism, photographers began to follow the model characterised most eloquently by Ralph Gibson, by becoming non-commercial. The idea of the photographer as poet had existed for almost a century, but such artists were rare, exotic creatures, like Fenton, Frith and Cameron. In no other artistic field, save possibly architecture, was the level of debate and excitement as ambitious or messianic as in the world of art photography.

At the height of this activity, Bailey launched *Ritz* magazine, a shameless English version of Andy Warhol's *Interview*. It was a typical gesture of the restless Bailey to throw a commercial fashion- and beauty-orientated spanner into the contemplative world of 'serious photography'. A new generation of fashion photographers grew out of *Ritz*, an event that lasted less than a decade. This, combined with the hot-bed of photographic creativity which centred around an art school in Nottingham (Trent Polytechnic, under the brilliant direction of Paul Hill), created a unique climate for the development of the medium in Britain.

Brian Clarke
London
1981

Andy Earl was a student at Trent at this time and was exposed directly to the work and teaching of Hill, Thomas Joshua Cooper, Gibson, Mary Ellen Mark and every other great American photographer that Paul Hill could bribe, bully or charm into coming to the rustic hills of the Peak District. It was in this atmosphere of creative contrasts that Andy Earl cut his teeth. On one side, he had the religious fervour of an academic institution pioneering a new art; and, on the other, the overwhelming glamour of the works of fashion, music and advertising, as summed up in the pages of *Ritz*.

The son of two Sussex doctors, Andy Earl is part of a tradition of English eccentric boffins, which marks him as quite different from his American counterparts. In his youth, just like his father, Earl surrounded himself with mechanical paraphernalia: motorbike parts, ancient engines of no particular origin, cars in various stages of decay and, at one time, a flat-bottomed barge anchored in a Nottinghamshire canal that flooded regularly. It was aboard this veteran craft of the Dunkirk evacuation that Earl lived when I first met him. He was something of a star student, already distinguished as the author of the now famous 'Ascot' pictures, the grotesqueries of the English upper class at play. The polar counterpart of Richard Billingham's recent book, *Ray's A Laugh*, in harmony with his photographs, Earl's pictures are non-judgemental. The subjects say everything themselves and the viewer is free to arrive at his own conclusions.

The meditative frame of mind that generally gives birth to the investigative, artistic pursuits of art photography intrigued Earl but failed to excite him. He wanted to engage the world full-frontally. The heady, challenging, daily demands of fashion and music made him hungry for change, and within a very short time span he had taken his enthusiasms for art photography into the world of commerce, at first for small provincial magazines and clients, and later to the zenith of popular culture and entertainment. Few of the principal figures of British and American popular music have eluded Earl's lens in the last 20 years.

Throughout this time, Earl had supported an active interest in contemporary architecture. He lives with his family in the seminal high-tech house known as 'Eagle Rock', a home designed by Ian Ritchie for an aged botanist at the same time that Earl was taking his 'Ascot' pictures. It's a pursuit that has led to the buildings of Norman Foster, Future Systems,

Richard Rogers and, lately, Oscar Niemeyer featuring prominently in his work. For many people across the world, Earl's views of the Niemeyer Niteroi Museum, depicted on the group ABC's CD cover, remain the main published exposure of this great building.

His videos and stills have drawn from such a great variety of influences that a chronicle of his *oeuvre* is, in itself, a useful document in the cataloguing of physical change that the built environment has witnessed in the same period of time.

It is his limitless enthusiasm and remarkable willingness to enter new territory that makes Andy Earl a photographer of interest, and it is his eagerness to share his discoveries, without judgement or cynicism, that makes him remarkable.

Yellow Dress
Ascot
1977

Eaay
Henley
1977

Introduction
Adrian Deevoy, London

Andy Earl is showing me a photograph by the American artist Ralph Gibson. It is a tightly-cropped black and white picture of a crisply-ironed shirt sleeve, rolled just above the elbow. The person wearing the shirt looks like a waitress. It strikes me that she might be Vietnamese but it's hard to say because you can only see her chin. There are hills on half the horizon with a few small clouds darting across them.

'This image is what made me want to get into photography,' Earl says with a barely-contained passion. 'Everything about it was so simple yet so mysterious. Was it a man or a woman? You knew it was a shirt but it could be a mountain range. It was so sharp it became abstract. It worked on so many levels. When I first saw this, the hairs on the back of my neck stood up.'

In normal circumstances I wouldn't mention this but Andy Earl recently took a photograph that had the same effect on me. It's a simple enough snap of what I fancy to be an English lagoon. But stare at it for long enough and it can transport you through cornfields, into endless summer, through dreams, back to childhood. It is quite magical.

Earl proudly tells me that he now owns a print of the Ralph Gibson picture and it hangs in his home.

The photograph Andy Earl took was bought by the UK Post Office and used on their second class stamps. At 19p, it's arguably the most attractively-priced piece of art available anywhere. And the most portable. I make sure I'm always carrying one in my wallet.

When Andy Earl and I were first flung together on an assignment we didn't do a stroke, didn't so much as shift an F-stop, for four days. We were in Monte Carlo waiting for an exclusive audience with Prince. And, if we say so ourselves, we got pretty good at waiting.

At that point in Prince's career – he was on the cusp of changing his name to a sexually-confused squiggle – the small showman hadn't granted an interview or photo session for five years and he wasn't about to rush into it now. Prince was playing a long game but he hadn't reckoned on coming up against such stiff competition. We could wait for England. We could wait for ever.

Monte Carlo is the kind of town that likes to regularly remind you that it prefers its millionaires to be multi. Killing an hour a day in a casino soon adds up. And it can look terrible on your expenses.

We spent a lot of our wait-time laughing. At the prices; at the contemptuous waiters; at the gauche names on the yachts; at the ubiquity of the Chanel logo; at the startling number of gnarled, navy-blazered roués with a 22-year-old gold-digger on their arm. It might be so monied as to make Liechtenstein look shabby, but Monaco is a hilarious place to hang around.

To keep up appearances, we attended a music awards ceremony where the only criterion for winning an award seemed to be showing up. We spent the rest of the night in a fascinatingly awful disco with the late and lovely Michael Hutchence, his then-girlfriend Helena Christensen and fellow supermodel Christy Turlington. Kylie Minogue was there too. And Prince. And Prince Albert of Monaco. That might sound like a too-fabulous-to-be-true crew but the evening had an almost intimate feel to it. Despite the fact that four drinks cost just over £90 we all got pleasantly drunk and, when the vast bill finally settled in front of us, Hutchence memorably suggested we either claim it or frame it.

There was sadness too. The evening after we arrived, Ayrton Senna crashed and died during the San Marino Grand Prix. Earl, a devoted disciple of motor racing, felt the tragedy deeply. The following morning we found ourselves consoling a devastated Michael Schumacher, who was walking around his adopted neighbourhood in a despondent daze, having lost his close friend. He was accompanied by a small, sad-looking dog, which was somehow unbearably poignant.

So we laughed, we cried but mostly we waited. In cafes, in bars, in the lobbies of snobby hotels. We also walked a lot. Around the streets of Monte Carlo, up to the highest point in the principality and back down again. And we talked, not of the job in hand as the circumstances were well beyond our control, but about how our lives had led us here.

By total fluke, was Earl's reassuringly-frank assessment of his career trajectory thus far. He had without doubt created and taken chances. He freely admitted that there had never been a strategy and the only plan he had was to periodically throw away the plan.

As Andy Earl told me his story, five random details stuck in my mind: he used to smoke roll-ups; he'd once worked as a mechanic for Formula One playboy James Hunt; he lived in a glass house previously owned by a botanist; he was mildly obsessed with surveying landscapes; and his youngest daughter had recently asked him, 'Dad, what's the muddiest you've ever been?'

After 96 hours in Monaco, Prince's people finally found a window in their airtight schedule. The shoot was due to take place on the roof of the Hotel De Paris at 5pm but Prince was already an hour late and Andy was in a dilemma as to whether he should use the fading natural daylight or fall back on flash. He set up lights anyway but, as cruel fortune would have it, the moment Prince arrived on the roof in full stage costume and make-up, a freak gust of wind swept in from the ocean and blew the Norman flash over. It crashed to the deck, showering the floor with broken glass. Hence Prince's first words, as he crunched across the shattered shards in his high heels, were, 'What the fuck's going on?' It wasn't the ideal start to any shoot but, astonishingly, Andy Earl remained calm.

The session lasted three minutes in its entirety. For one frame, Prince waved his hand mysteriously in front of his face. 'You're taking the piss, aren't you?' Andy asked, clicking furiously. 'And you've just got your shot,' replied Prince and the ordeal was over.

Five years. Four days. Three minutes. Two rolls of film. One superb magazine cover. This Andy Earl was the sort of unflappable bloke you wanted to work with.

For our next job, Andy and myself were commissioned to join REM on tour in Barcelona. Our brief was to capture the hysteria, insanity and megalomania of a planet-straddling rock band at the height of their powers.

I would be the first to admit that I failed in my attempt to get to the heart of the beast on that particular story. Access to the central figures was limited, the itinerary prohibitively restrictive and spirits were low. I wanted to write about the sacrifices a band has to make in order to gain a premier league promotion. How they must relinquish control while creating the illusion of power. How you might feel on top of the world but your fans think you've sold them out and your friends think you are a tosser. I couldn't do it. Infuriatingly, Andy managed to capture these complex emotions in one hastily-grabbed photograph.

His session with Michael Stipe was another swift one – no more than ten minutes in length – but that single image of the furrow-browed singer looking simultaneously bored, superior, baffled and knowing seemed to sum up the entire feeling of the tour. The crowning glory was the question mark on Stipe's hat which, in many ways, spoke for us all. What were we doing there? What was going on? And, more pertinently, when could we go home?

Earl's impressive hit rate made me determined to blow my new colleague's cool. Some months later, whilst interviewing Elton John in London, just moments before Andy was due to photograph him, I asked the tantrum-prone pianist if, during his wilder years, he had ever rubbed cocaine into his penis. Elton handled the question very well. Andy, however, lost his nerve. 'I couldn't believe it,' he laughs now. 'I just assumed he would end the interview there and then, cancel the shoot and flounce out. I started packing my gear away. I assumed I would now be surplus to requirements.'

Needless to say, the shoot went ahead – Elton in a pink plastic suit, eating chips out of a copy of The Sun newspaper, if memory serves – and Andy Earl chalked up another visually-stylish yet journalistically-intelligent cover for Q magazine. He's annoying like that.

Michael Stipe
Barcelona
1995

Elton John
London
1995

Bow Wow Wow
Dejeuner Sur L'Herbe
1981

Eaay
Henley
1977

Barbecue Chicken
1977

When asked to pinpoint the reason he takes photographs, Andy Earl looks calmly into the middle distance, thinks for a moment and says, 'For me, it's about getting that visual fix.' His craving for this aesthetic opiate began, he claims, when he spent a year in Baltimore during the early Seventies. 'They were all shooting their art photography in colour, which I love,' he explains. 'Britain was still very into meaningful black and white but I was full of this idea that you should shoot in colour. The problem was when I came back to Britain, I found the lighting was very dull and the pictures were just drab, so I started putting a flash on the camera to intensify the colours. Then, by accident, I set the camera wrongly and got this weird blurring effect.'

Without realising that he'd hit upon a technique that would become his trademark, he christened the system 'flash and blur' and put it to the test in the unlikely environs of Ascot races and Henley Regatta. Here he stalked the English aristocracy with an enormous old plate camera and a massive flash, barbecuing every be-hatted toff in sight. If anyone questioned his credentials he simply replied, 'Tatler,' and fired off another cheeky frame.

It was at this time that Earl took what has become one of his most celebrated photographs. It is a shot, let's not mince our words, of a chicken's arse. It's an arresting image, alive with colour and crackling with energy but, as is often the case in Earlworld, it was a complete accident.

'I was actually trying to take a photo of a girl in Chatsworth Park,' he laughs. 'She was lying on the grass, it had an almost Pre-Raphaelite feel to it and there were these chickens wandering around which I thought would add a bit of colour. As I went to take the shot, I tripped over one of the leads, the shutter went off and I got this funny, blurred picture of a chicken's behind. Of course, everyone at college loved it. They thought it was art.'

In many senses, it was. The chicken shot was exhibited at the prestigious Venice Biennale in 1979 and it is no coincidence that David Bailey still insists on admiringly calling Earl 'Chickenshit'.

Meanwhile, the intriguing sharp-but-smudged shots Earl had taken at Ascot led to an exhibition at the Photographers' Gallery in London. The show was attended by, amongst others, slippery punk entrepreneur Malcolm McLaren who, impressed by the painterly quality of Earl's work, promptly offered

him a session with his latest charges – a band called Bow Wow Wow.

'The idea was to copy the Manet painting "Dejeuner Sur L'Herbe",' says Earl. 'So I went off to find a bit of river in Surrey which didn't have a council estate in the background and I eventually found this lake, with a tiny island, in a park in Reigate. I was amazed because it was almost identical to the Manet. So we set up the shoot, the band all turned up dressed in Vivienne Westwood's pirate gear and it was only then that I discovered that no-one had told Annabella, the singer, what the concept was: that she had to take her clothes off. She was only 14 and there she was, sitting there very coyly, starkers, and at this point the entire local primary school processed past on a nature walk!' He breaks off in peals of uncontrollable laughter before gathering himself and finishing the anecdote. 'Everybody loved the shots, apart from Annabella's mother who contacted the police and I had to hand over the negatives. Well, most of them.'

The Bow Wow Wow shot, nicknamed 'Only in it for the Manet', came to define an era. This was the start of the Eighties and New Romance was in the air. Earl's next project was to photograph a rumbling lot from Birmingham who turned out to be Duran Duran. 'They were so unknown and I was so naive,' Earl says, 'that I put John Taylor at the front of the set-up because he was the prettiest. I didn't know that you were supposed to put the singer up front. I wasn't a music fan at all, I was just interested in taking a nice picture.'

Surprisingly, for someone who is routinely described as 'music's foremost photographer' and, even more appallingly, 'rock's top lensman', Earl isn't a music fanatic. When he photographed Martin Fry amid the astonishing futurist Sixties architecture of Brasilia, it was more for the reason that he loved the city's timeless quality and admired Fry as a man than the fact that he was a hopeless ABC devotee.

Although Andy Earl is always more likely to say, 'Look what the sky is doing there' than, 'I wonder how they got the snare sound on this?' he remains the pop photographer they ask for by name. When visionary director Michel Gondry came up with the idea of shooting a video for The Rolling Stones using still photographs morphed together, Earl was his immediate choice.

'I had never done anything like it before,' Earl shrugs. 'I don't think anyone had. I turned up on the first day of the shoot and it was a big budget production – everyone was in their separate Winnebago – and one of the production guys came over and said, "Andy, do you think this is going to work?" and I said, "I honestly haven't got a clue." Obviously I'd planned it all out and taken test shots based on the Ascot technique, but it was still high risk. Then the head of lighting asked me what lights I'd need and I said, "Well, I'm just using the flash on the camera" and he looked a bit disappointed so I said, "I might need a bit of tracing paper as well."'

During the four-day shoot, Earl worked like a flash-driven dervish, rotating five camera bodies all fitted with bulky 250-frame backs. He took 12,000 pictures in all which meant superhuman levels of concentration – not to mention a monumental amount of admin – but the results are an intoxicating, dimension-defying triumph.

'When I started using the flash and blur it made the whole effect come to life,' he enthuses. 'It gave everything a softness and a rhythm and a blurry, sexy, druggy feel which suited the legend of The Rolling Stones. My wife Sophie came down to the set and she was watching the band perform the song and she looked down at Mick Jagger's trousers and thought to herself, "My, he does look well endowed – it's true what they say." Then Jagger reached into his pocket and pulled out a harmonica. I was so busy rattling off shots I didn't even notice. But I loved every heart-pounding minute of the shoot and I'm extremely pleased with the end result.'

Indeed. 'Like A Rolling Stone' won Earl a D&AD award for Best Video in 1996.

Keith Richards
Gondry Video, London
1995

Mick Jagger
Gondry Video, London
1995

Everyone has got a bit of Andy Earl in them. Root through your record collection and you'll stumble upon at least one of his mini-masterworks. If you own albums by Boyzone, Eurythmics, Pink Floyd, The Lightning Seeds, Duran Duran or The Manic Street Preachers, you could inadvertently be hosting a private exhibition of Andy Earl's photography.

Earl's instantly memorable and insidiously classic album covers have become his stock-in-trade. He would be loath to tell you this, but in 1997 the best-selling UK album was Robbie Williams' *Life Thru A Lens*. Cover shot: Andy Earl. In 1998, the best-selling UK album was *This Is My Truth, Tell Me Yours*. Andy Earl again. In 1999, the best-selling UK album was *Boyzone – By Request*. The photographer? You're getting the picture.

'Actually the Boyzone shoot was a nightmare,' says Earl humbly. 'It was drizzling relentlessly in Dublin, as it does, so to get any kind of atmosphere I had to light the entire street and it still looked flat. The next morning I went back and it was bathed in this beautiful diffused sunlight. So I took a shot of that and went back to London and fudged it all together on a computer. Sometimes you have to resort to technology when nature lets you down.'

'For the Manics cover,' he continues, 'the idea was to make North Wales look like Nebraska. No small feat. We wanted something that was really honest and the location had to have a certain clarity to it. You wouldn't have thought Harlech Beach would give you that but it did. The only real problem was getting three people to stand on a beach without them feeling like idiots, and that really came down to them just being comfortable with each other, and then trusting me enough to relax and be themselves.'

This is the principal reason these heavily-platinumed artists choose to collaborate with Andy Earl: they trust him, they like his methods and they love the results.

Robbie Williams remembers working with Andy Earl as 'a doddle, no ego involved – apart from mine, of course. He got there, did the job, shook hands and left. Why can't all photographers be like that?' The concept for *Life Thru A Lens* was a courtroom steps pageant highlighting the press-hounded pop star as a jubilant victor. 'Funnily enough,' says Williams, "that was me being vindicated pre-vindication, if you know what I

mean. So not only is he a great photographer but he can see into the future, too.'

And just as every picture tells a story, every picture, inevitably, has a story behind it. Whether it was making up Courtney Love while she lay unconscious on a studio floor; being paid a pittance for shooting the poster for *Four Weddings And A Funeral*; securing a lucrative gig with Deutsche Bank because they liked your Robbie Williams shot; trying to locate a McDonald's in the frozen wastes of Iceland in order to placate a pair of peckish rappers; or attaching fishing weights to birds' wings and discussing light bulb fittings with Spanish customs officers all in the name of Pink Floyd. Oh, and Duran Duran's video for 'Hungry Like The Wolf" features two nuns. Andy Earl is the stubblier of the sisters.

'It's been completely surreal,' Earl confesses. 'Even more surreal when you consider that I wanted to be a fashion photographer.'

Four Weddings And A Funeral
London
1994

Robbie Williams
London
1997

Manic Street Preachers
Wales
1998

Boyzone
Ireland
1999

It's a chilly spring afternoon and Andy Earl, the failed fashion photographer, is sipping broccoli soup on the sofa of his studio in Butler's Wharf. A century ago, these riverside warehouses were used by the spice traders to store their fragrant cargo and the breeze still carries pungent undernotes of Keralan cardamom and sweet Grenadian nutmeg. These days, of course, you're more likely to run into an unscrupulous property developer than a broken-toothed smuggler, but it is comforting to look to the top of the street where the Thames obliviously goes about its mighty business.

We're sifting through Andy's work, discussing the characters, the technicalities, the concepts, the pure delight and the sheer absurdity of the modern photographer's life.

'I'm always nervous before a shoot,' he says, setting down his soup. 'I think that's a good thing because the adrenaline keeps you on your toes. If I go in there and I'm too cocky, I blow it. The Madonna shoot I did was very nerve-wracking, not because of her, but because of the whole circus that came with her. There were 40 people in the hotel room: friends, a film crew, make-up artists, managers, managers' assistants, managers' assistants' assistants. So it was tense. She was nervous because she didn't know me. I was nervous because I'd never met her. It's always good to have met someone before, just to see how they move or if they have any particular mannerisms that would look good. But because of the number of people in the room there was very little communication. In retrospect, I should have taken charge and kicked a lot of the people out but, then again, that might have created an atmosphere. So it was difficult. But that wasn't the real problem: I'd just bought these new boots and my feet were so hot – it's always the little things you remember. But I got a lovely shot of Madonna screaming. She went to the window and there were hundreds of fans outside screaming her name and she turned back to the room mimicking them. So I got a nice image there.'

This is a typical Andy Earl recollection of an encounter with a celebrity. While other photo-graphers are content to share the superstar's rarefied air and shoot their best side, Earl is forever studying the scene, searching for that tiny detail that will elevate the shot into the realm of the extra-ordinary. As Terence Donovan always said, there are a lot of photographers who can take good pictures but only a few can capture that little bit of magic.

Morrissey
USA
1995

Johnny Cash
Australia
1994

'I try to transcend straight portraiture,' Earl says. 'I always pull back and look for the bigger picture.'

It is in doing this that Earl often produces his most beguiling work. In his exquisite panoramic picture of Morrissey draped on the Los Angeles Observatory wall, it is the torque between the 'To Telescope' sign pointing west and his handsome subject's jutting chin and quiff facing east that makes it so compelling. Upon seeing the photo for the first time Morrissey, a master of understatement, sighed and said, 'It's really rather beautiful, isn't it?'

Similarly Earl's apocalyptic depiction of Johnny Cash, flanked by two dogs, on a Godforsaken roadside beneath an unforgiving sky, is so skilfully revealing because it shows a tough but tender soul. A man in the September of his life, at one with the cruel elements, the hungry hounds and the weight of the world.

'He's a big, imposing, authoritarian, very gruff character,' Earl recalls. 'And his face is like a geographical map, lines everywhere, completely weather-beaten with these piercing, virtually black eyes. I wanted a picture of him on the road with his guitar case – a journeyman-type idea. I tried it but it wasn't working. Then these clouds came up over the horizon and, because he was dressed in black and looked like a preacherman I said, "Let's just try something in front of a wheat field." As we did, the dogs, who belonged to the local stationmaster, came up and sat next him but one wouldn't stay put, so I said to Johnny Cash, "Could you try and make him sit?" And, wham, with one movement of his hand he got the dog to sit. And that was the picture. Shot done. All the elements came together. It's a portrait in its own right but the environment is as important because it tells you the whole story. The face, the sky, the field, the dogs. It's rather spiritual.'

Translate, transform, transcend. This is *Vista* by Andy Earl. Drink it in. It's rather spiritual.

PM Dawn
Iceland
1991

Homage to Ralph Gibson
Beachy Head, England
1999

Amar
Beachy Head, England
1999

Bow Wow Wow
Dejeuner Sur L'Herbe
1981

Mick Jagger
England
1987

Deutsche Bank
Baltimore, USA
1999

Dario G
Thailand
1998

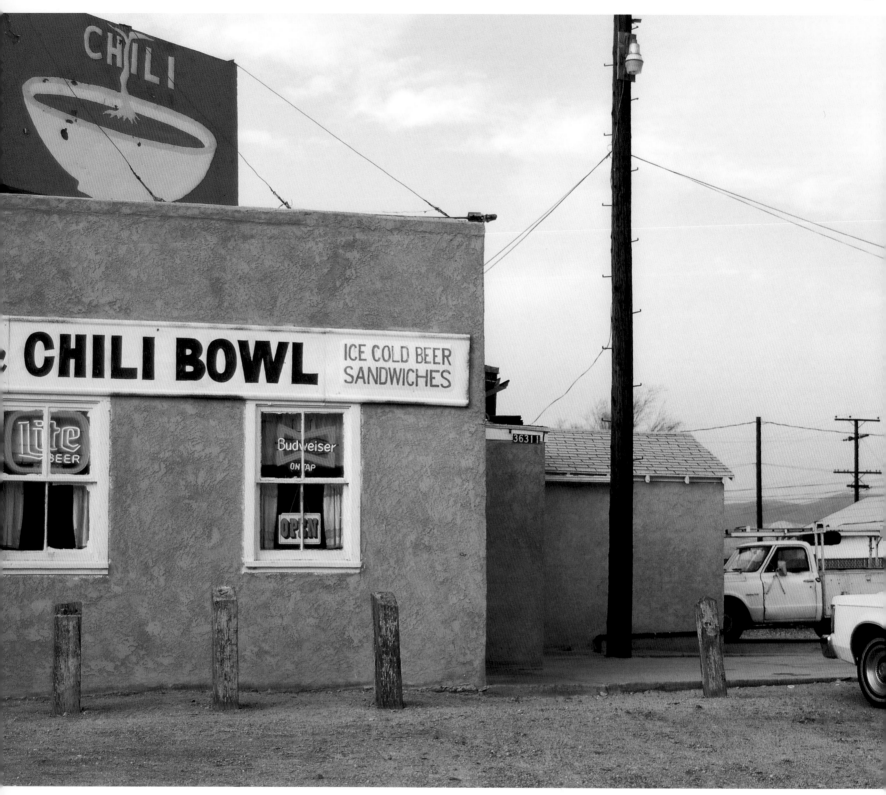

Chili Bowl
USA
1995

Nan
Mojave Desert, USA
1991

Dave Stewart
USA
1991

Paint Me Down
London
1984

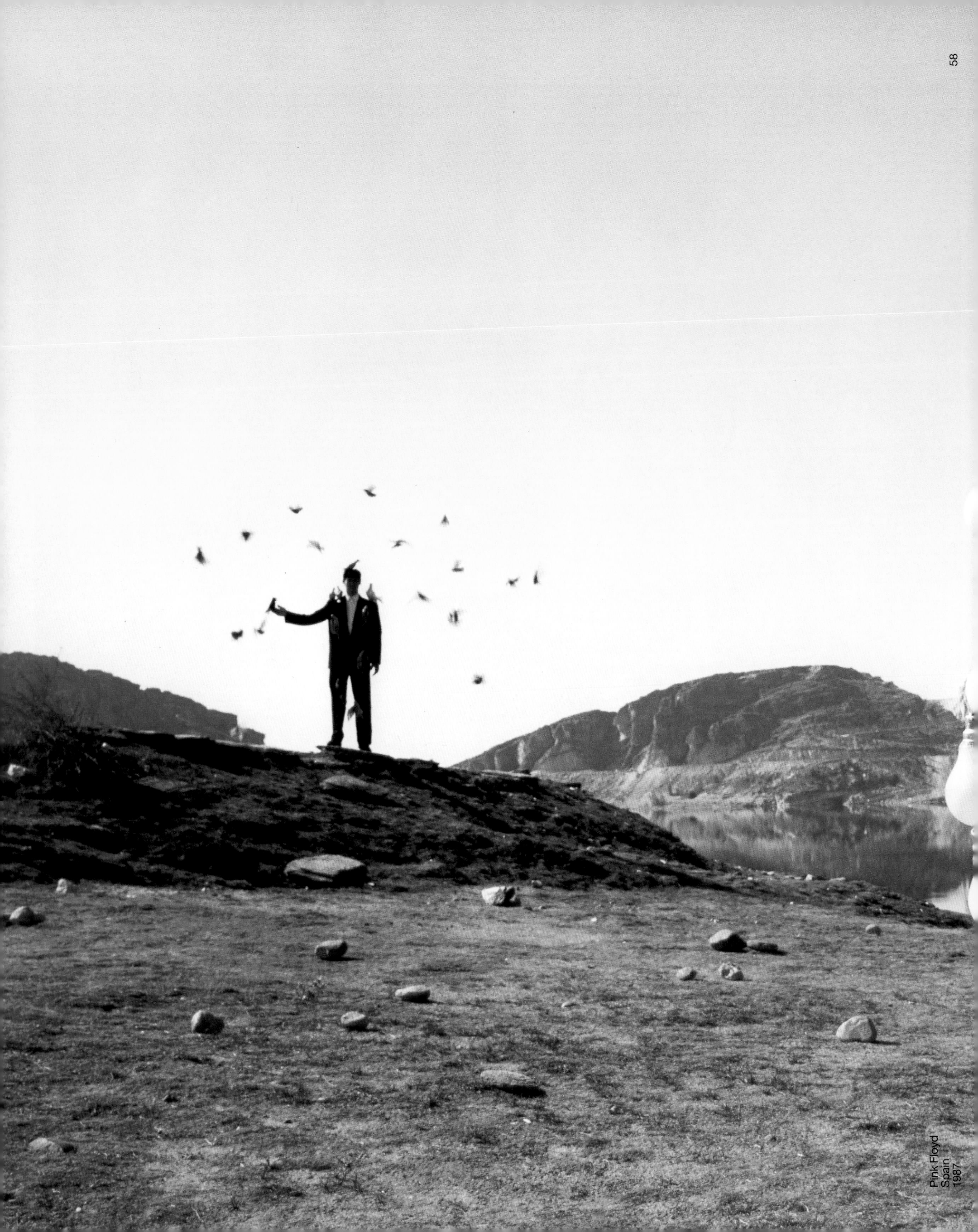

Pink Floyd
Spain
1987

Robbie Williams
London
1997

Madonna
Paris
1994

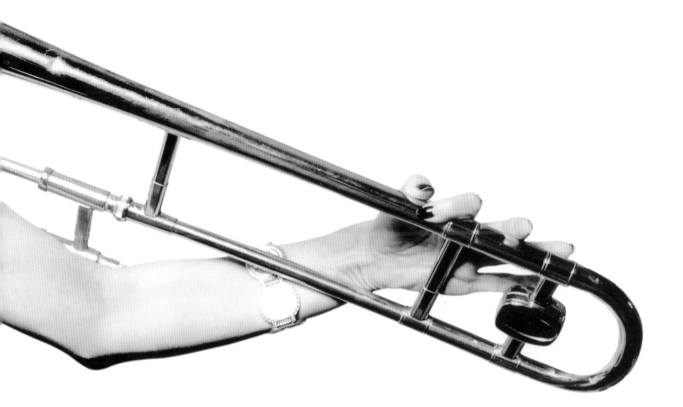

Trading Floor
London
1999

Morcheeba
London
2000

Manic Street Preachers
Wales
1998

Natalie Imbruglia
Barcelona
1997

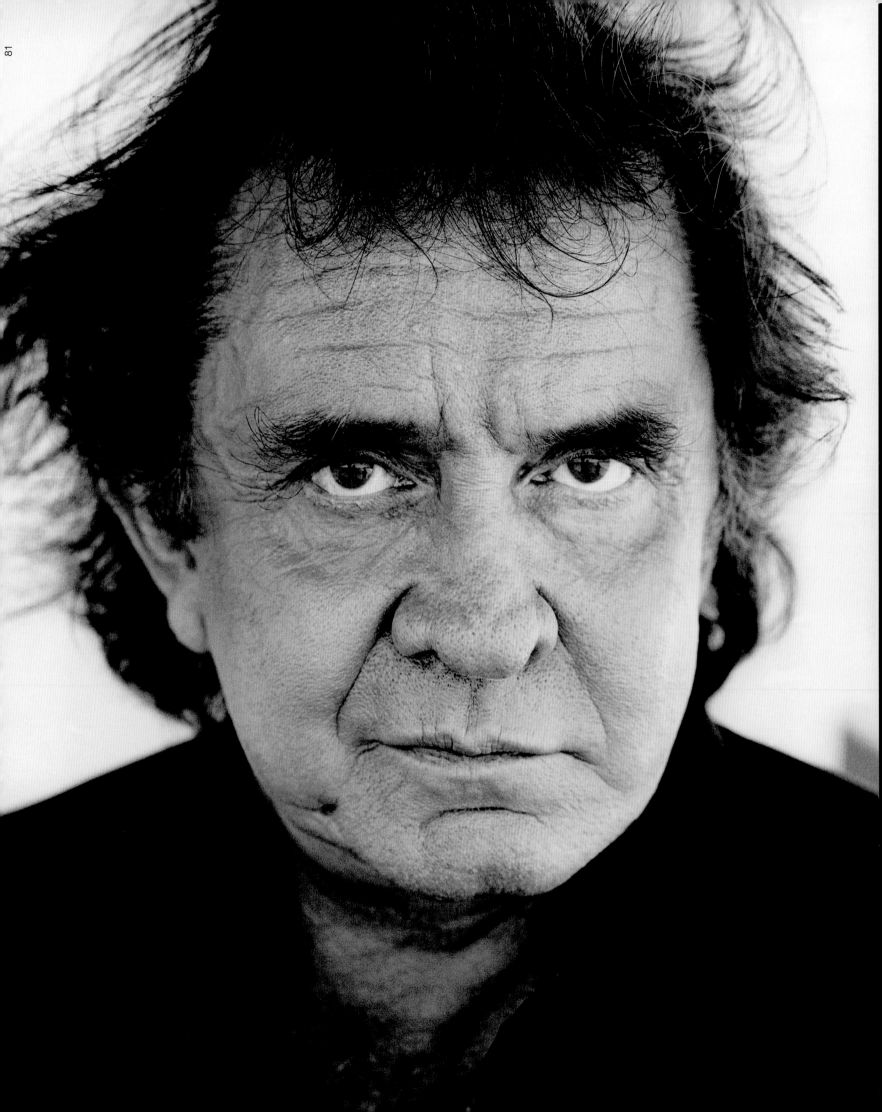

Keep Clean
USA
1995

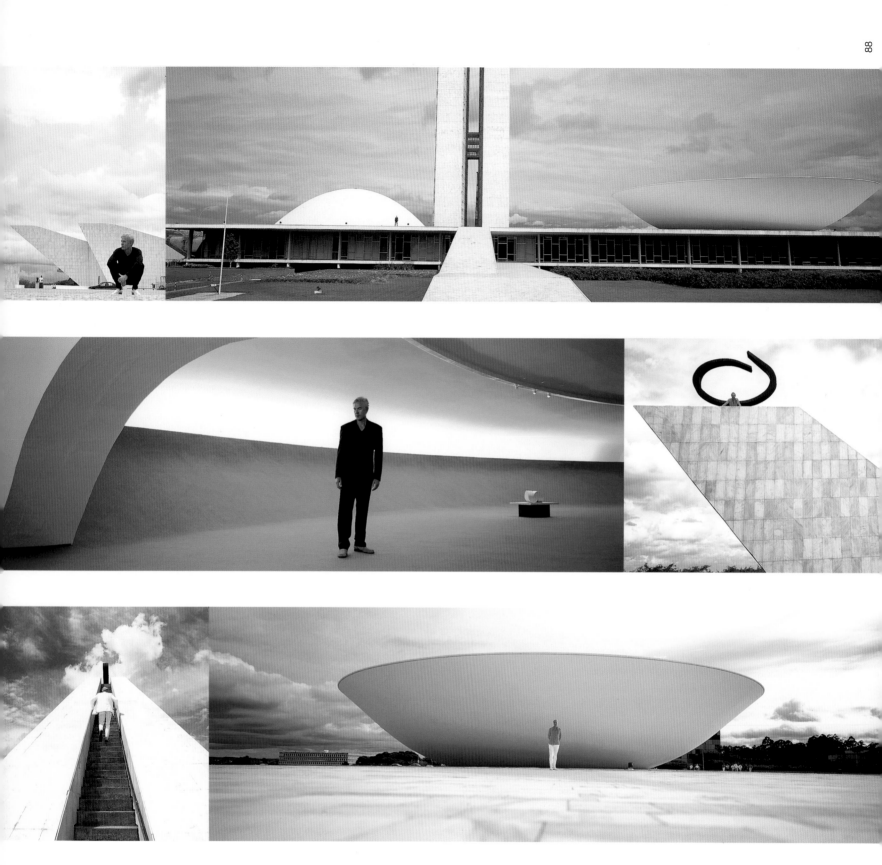

ABC
Brasilia and Rio De Janeiro
1997

Courtney Love
New York
1995

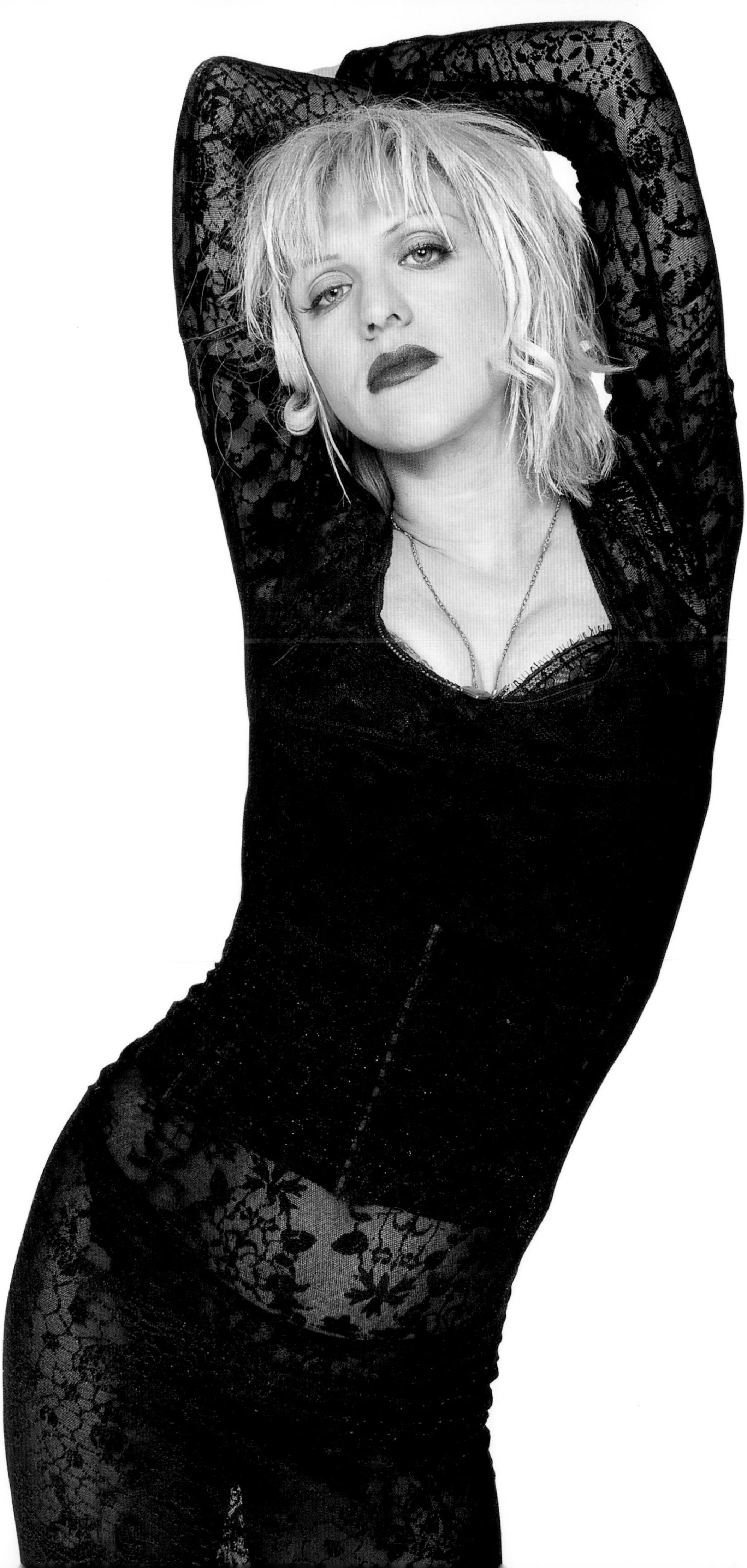

Stamp
England
2000

Mayte (Mrs Prince)
London
1995

Alison Limerick
France
1993

Alison Limerick
France
1993

Paul Weller
London
1996

Carl Macintosh
Virgin Islands
1990

Chicken
England
1978

Annie Lennox
Paris
1991

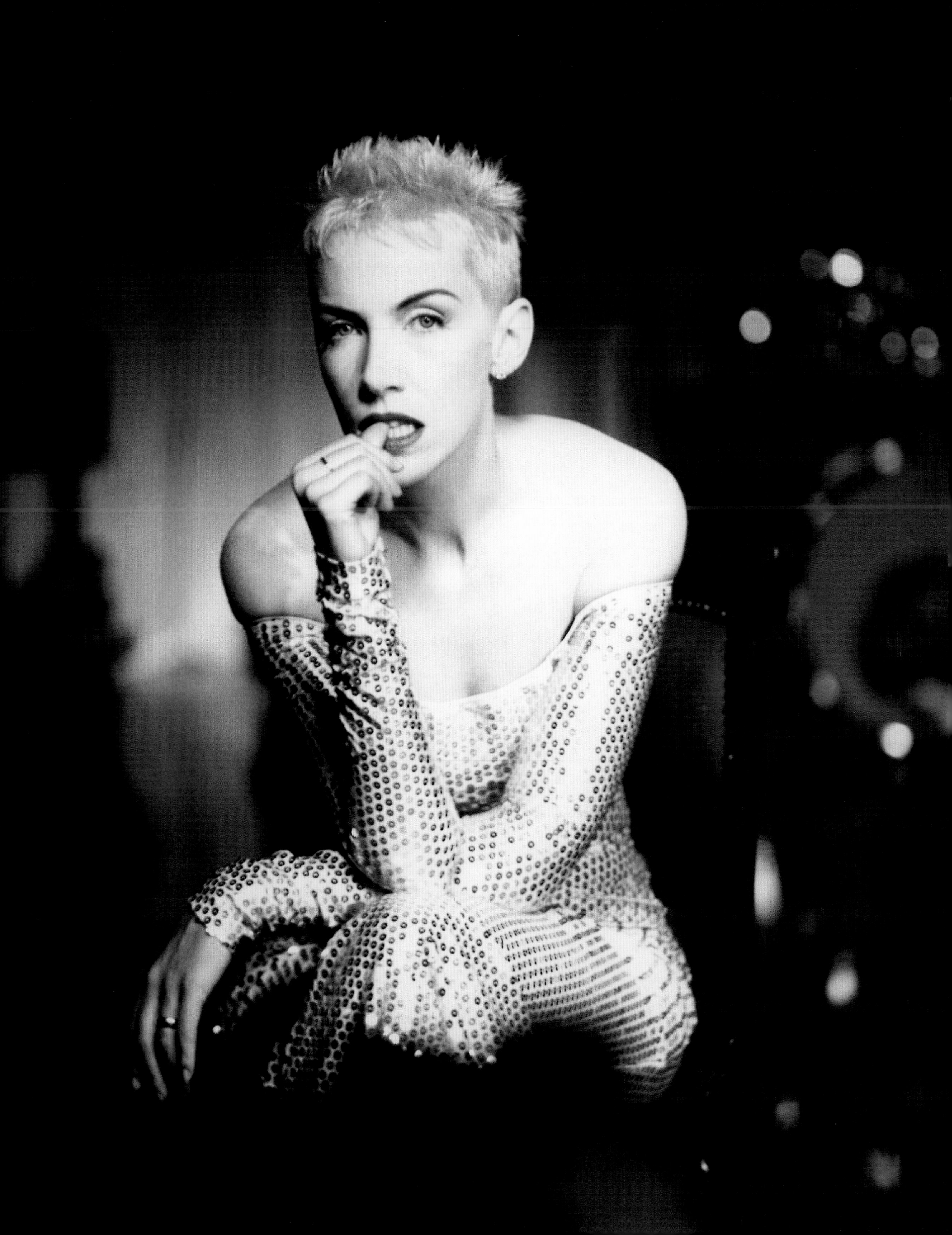

Manic Street Preachers
Wales
1998

Alanis Morissette
Utah
1996

Crowded House
New Zealand
1996

Michael Stipe
Barcelona
1995

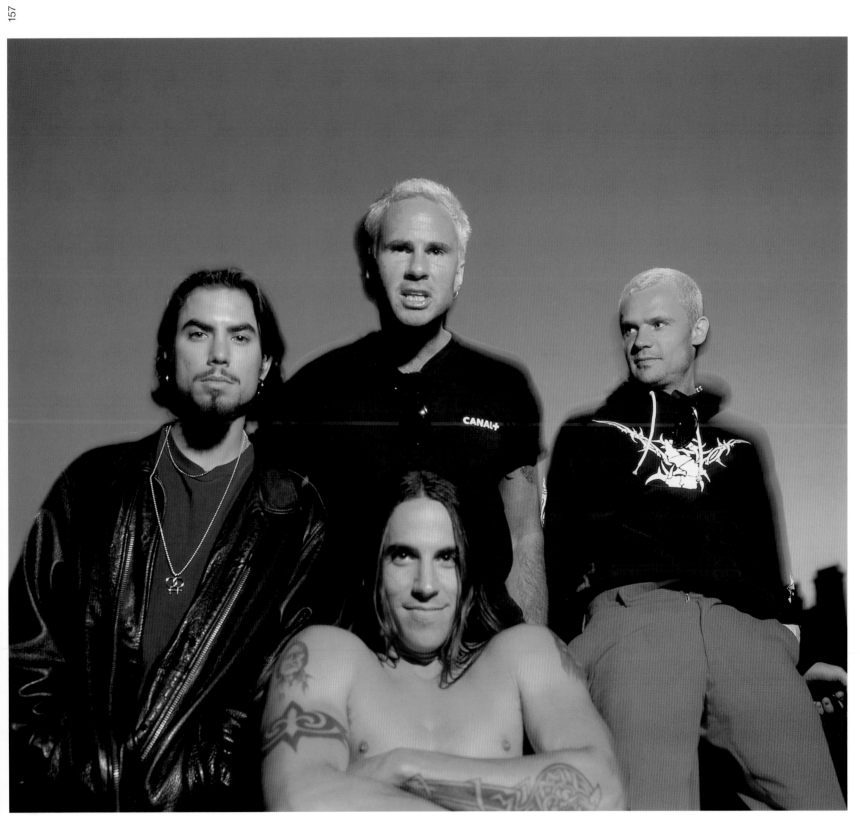

Soho
London
1998

Robbie Williams
London
1997

Goose
England
1985

4–5

6–7

8–9

10–11

27

28–29

30–31

32–33

42–43

45

46–47

48–49

58–59

61

62–63

64–65

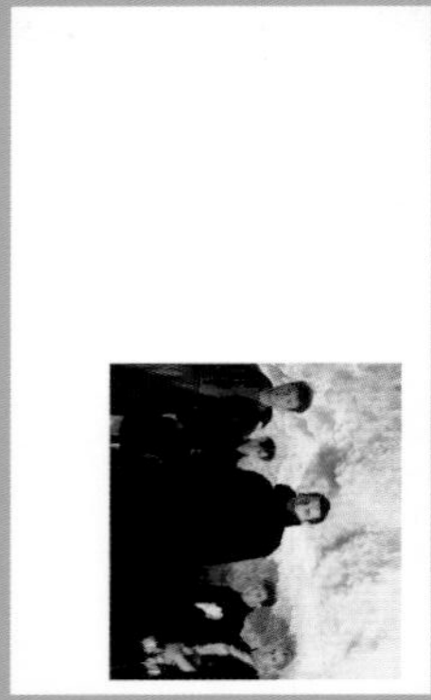

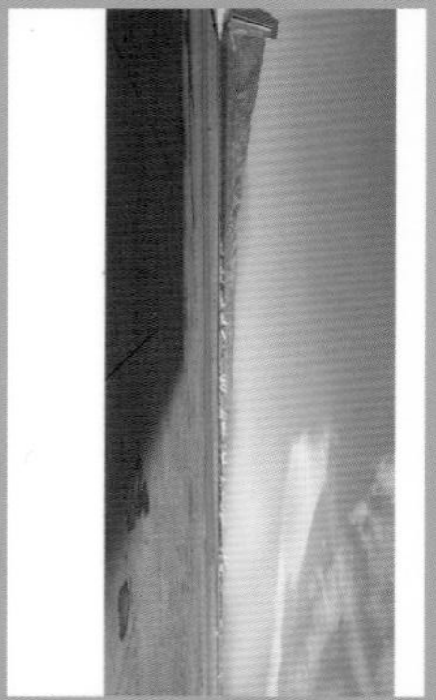

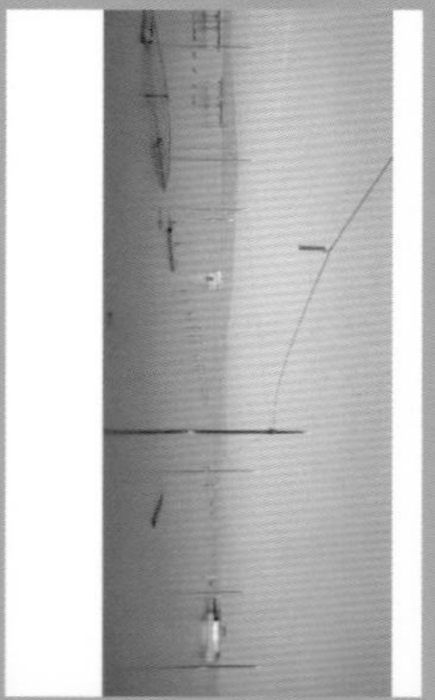

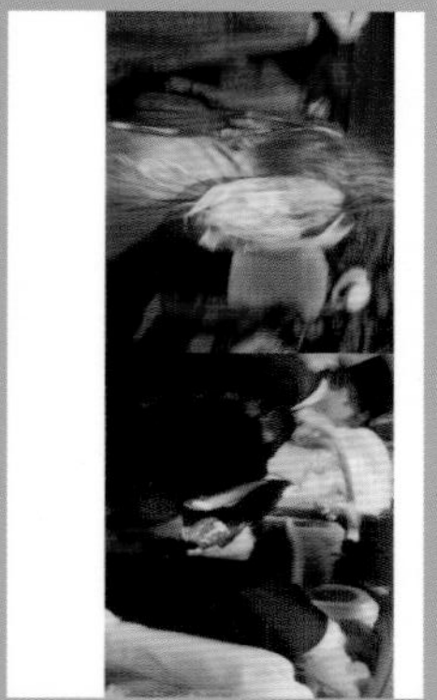

12–13

14–21

23

24–25

34–35

37

38–39

41

50–51

52–53

54–55

56–57

66–67

68–69

71

72–73

45
Travis, Scotland, 1999

46–47
Simon Le Bon, London, 1983
Design: Malcolm Garett. EMI Records.

48
Jarvis Cocker, Stockholm, 1996

49
Damon Albarn, London, 1996

50–51
Dario G, Thailand, 1998

52–53
Chili Bowl, USA, 1995

54
Nan, Mojave Desert, USA, 1991

55
Dave Stewart, USA, 1991
I was sitting back to front on another of Dave's Harleys. Afterwards, my driver said, 'That's the first time I've ever taken a passenger.'

56
Spandau Ballet, London, 1984

57
Paint Me Down, London, 1984
The song was called 'Paint Me Down' so we did. Video shoot with Russell Mulcahy. Chrysalis Records.

58–59
Pink Floyd, Spain, 1987
Yes, there are six people from Animal Actors behind the rocks, launching doves on the count of three. First major encounter with Storm Thorgerson. EMI Records EMKA.

61
Robbie Williams, London, 1997

62–63
Robbie Williams, London, 1997
Behind the pillars are a battery of flashes so when Robbie jumped unaided the intense backlight caught him mid-air. Design: Matt Cooke at Intro. Chrysalis Records.

64–65
Madonna, Paris, 1994
A play on James Dean's Rebel Without A Cause. And in answer to the question – yes, she is really nice. Thanks to Madonna, Barbara Cherone, Liz Rosenburg.

66–67
Trading Floor, London, 1999

68–69
Dario G, Thailand, 1998
We found a sandy ridge at low tide, dug mirrors into the sand and ended up with a visual interpretation of the title, 'Sunmachine'. Warner Records.

71
Morcheeba, London, 2000
In search of the surreal, I used mirrors at the recently-opened Jubilee Line of the London Underground. East/West Records.

72–73
Scritti Politti, London, 1985
The gents' toilet of the Liberal Club. Design: Keith Breeden. Virgin Records.

74–75
Manic Street Preachers, Wales, 1998

76–77
Natalie Imbruglia, Barcelona, 1997
Natalie saw the Johnny Cash pictures in my portfolio and asked, 'Can I look like that?' 'Not a chance!' I said – but I think she liked the lith print. RCA Records.

79–81
Johnny Cash, Australia, 1994
Initial idea was Johnny walking down the railway – but it wasn't working. Storm clouds were rising over the fields; the stationmaster's dogs were running around. This is one of those shots where all the elements came together. Design: Martyn Atkins. Thanks Johnny Cash and American Recordings.

82–83
Keep Clean, USA, 1995

85
Sting, South Africa, 1995

86–91
ABC, Brasilia and Rio De Janeiro, 1997
The title was 'Skyscraping'. Mark Farrow has a fascination with Oscar Neimeyer's Brasilia. I also have a passion for modern architecture and, with Martin Fry's cooperation and constant running, we achieved this. Design: Farrow Design. Deconstruction Records.

93
Courtney Love, New York, 1995

94–95
Milkshake, England, 1978

97
Stamp, England, 2000
Having to move the camera so a cloud didn't interfere with the Queen's head… It was a wonderful job to be asked to do. Design: Pentagram Design. Royal Mail.

98–99
Loose Ends, Morocco, 1986

100–101
Another Level, New York, 1999

102–103
Jim Kerr, Spain, 1991

104–107
12,000 stills morphed together to produce the most exciting video I've been involved with. Thank you Michel Gondry, The Rolling Stones, Patricia Arquette and the production, Peter Chambers, Kathy Hood, loads of assistants and Virgin Records.

104–105
Patricia Arquette, Gondry Video, London, 1995

106–107
Keith Richards and Mick Jagger, Gondry Video, London, 1995

109
Mayte (Mrs Prince), London, 1995

110–111
Alison Limerick, France, 1993

172

82–83

85

86–87

88–89

98–99

100–101

102–103

104–105

114–115

116–117

118–119

120–121

131

132–133

135

136–137

112
Level 42, New Orleans, 1993

113
Paul Weller, London, 1996

114–115
Fish, Scotland, 1992
It's pouring with rain on the Isle of Lewis –
my assistant, Frankie, is cowering behind
the first standing stone with the inevitable
flash. Polydor Records.

116–117
Singapore, 1999

118
Carl McIntosh, Virgin Islands, 1990

119
Blow Monkeys, England, 1990

120–121
Chicken, England, 1978

122–123
Loose Ends, Sahara Desert, 1986
One of my first panoramic shots. By 6am
the sun was up and the dunes had lost
their glow and looked like concrete.
Design: Bill Smith. Virgin Records.

125
Annie Lennox, Paris, 1991
Annie was immersed in her own thoughts,
I caught her attention and she looked up –
one of my favourites. RCA Records.

126–127
Tricky, London, 1996

128–129
Manic Street Preachers, Wales, 1998

131
J Perkins, USA, 1991

132
Boyzone, Ireland, 1999

133
Ronan Keating, Ireland, 1999

135
Spiritual Cowboys, USA, 1991
As the sun goes down in the desert, there is
invariably a strong wind. We were packing
up a 'last supper' scene and I got all hands
on deck holding the banners.

136–137
Alanis Morissette, Utah, 1996

139

141

142–143

144–145

154–155

156–157

158–159

161

139–141
Cranberries, Monument Valley 1 and 2, 1999
Driving around Arizona with two enormous
plastic eyes, an assistant whipping his
clothes off and Storm asking, 'Can we try
it from this angle too?' Design: Storm
Thorgerson. Thanks to The Cranberries –
this is my fourth cover for them.
Island Records.

142–143
Audience, USA, 1991
Inspired by a Duane Hanson painting.

144–145
Salt & Ice, USA, 1995
The Colorado River had burst its banks,
flooding a salt mine valley. When the water
receded the salt had taken control.

147
Crowded House, New Zealand, 1996
On the beach where they filmed *The Piano*.
Design: Rob O'Connor. Parlophone Records.

148–149
Crowded House, New Zealand, 1996

150–151
UB40, France, 1993

152–153
Deutsche Bank, New York, 1999

154–155
Michael Stipe, Barcelona, 1995
As he jumped out of his car at the hotel,
I asked him to look straight at the setting
sun. Q magazine. Warner Records.

156
Cranberries, Ireland, 1999

157
Red Hot Chili Peppers, London, 1995

158–159
Soho, London, 1998

161
Robbie Williams, London, 1997
The Ascot confrontation. I connected the
photographer's flashes to my camera to
control the 'barbecued' paparazzi look.
Design: Matt Cooke. Chrysalis Records.

162–163
Tokyo, 1999

164–165
Goose, England, 1985

166
Eurythmics, Paris, 1991

167
Archive, London, 1998
We travelled all around England with lamps
and mirrors – and ended up taking this 50
metres from my studio. Design: Matt Cooke.
Island Records.

168–169
Morrissey, USA, 1995
As the sun went in, I reverted to flash – to
subtly bring him out from the background.
Q magazine.

147

148–149

150–151

152–153

162–163

164–165

166–167

168–169

I'd like to thank all the individual artists, record companies, management and designers for their support and enthusiasm in creating these pictures. I hope you enjoy them.

Hasta la Vista.

Family portrait

Acknowledgments:

Martyn Atkins
Debbie Baker
Barry Barnes
Stuart Batholomew
Tom Bird
Cally
Barbara Cherone
Tom Cooper
Simon Cowells
Shaun Higson
Paul Hill
Ted Humble-Smith
Idea
Danny Kelly
Frankie Lane
Elaine Macintosh
Julian Marsh
John McDowell
Jim McKay
Stuart McKenzie
Jamie Morgan
Adrian Myers
Rob O'Connor
Paula Pell-Johnson
Q
Hermione Ross
Ashley Rossitter
Bill Smith
Angus Stokes
Sally Stothard
Christian Tattershall
Storm Thorgerson
Jackie Tyson

Special thanks to:

Brian Clarke
Adrian Deevoy
Mark Farrow
Jonathon Jeffrey

and

Ali
Dan
Megan
Nina